AF226117

1 Yet Publishing

YETS!
ISBN: 9780578719351

For more information, please visit:
www.artistmb.com

First Edition

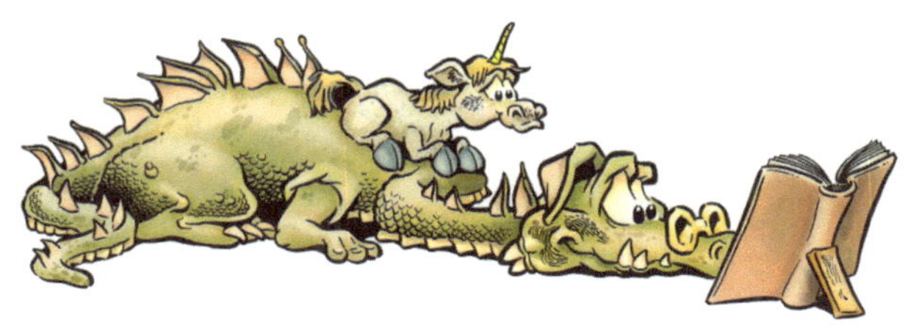

For Linda and Ondi

Howdy!

I must confess.
I did not create the Yets.
I was introduced to the Yets by a young Guinea Pig named Sir Perry.
Perry traveled with Yets for many years, and
he insisted that I tell you about his strange friends.
Are the Yets very different from us?
Are they strange?
I don't know.
I just draw whatever Perry tells me to draw.
You may answer those questions,
and tell Perry if you see him.

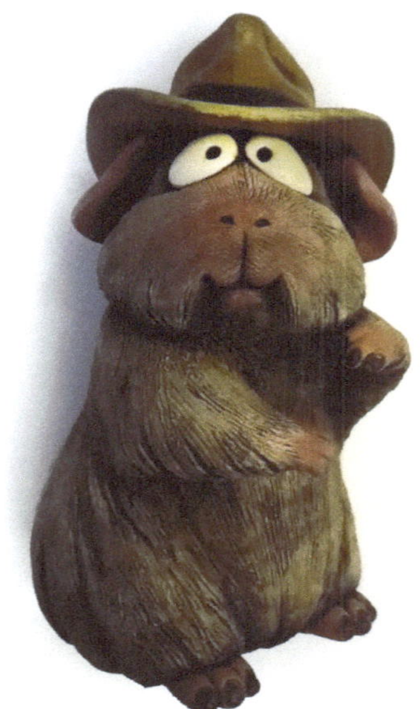

*Photo of Sir Perry The Adventuring Guinea Pig
used with permission from Perry's estate.*

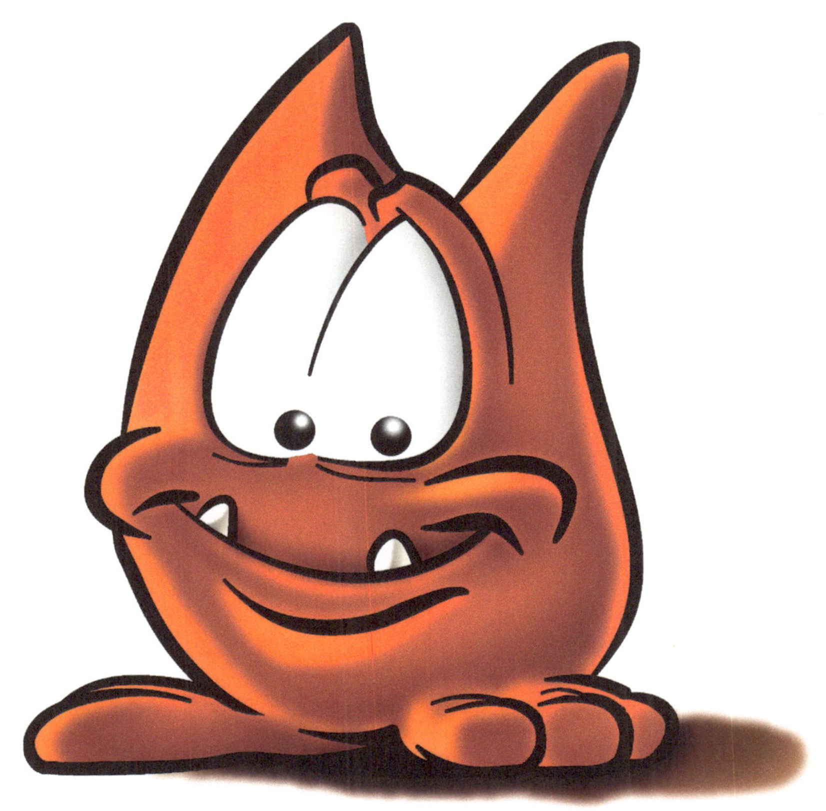

Here is a creature and Yet is its name.

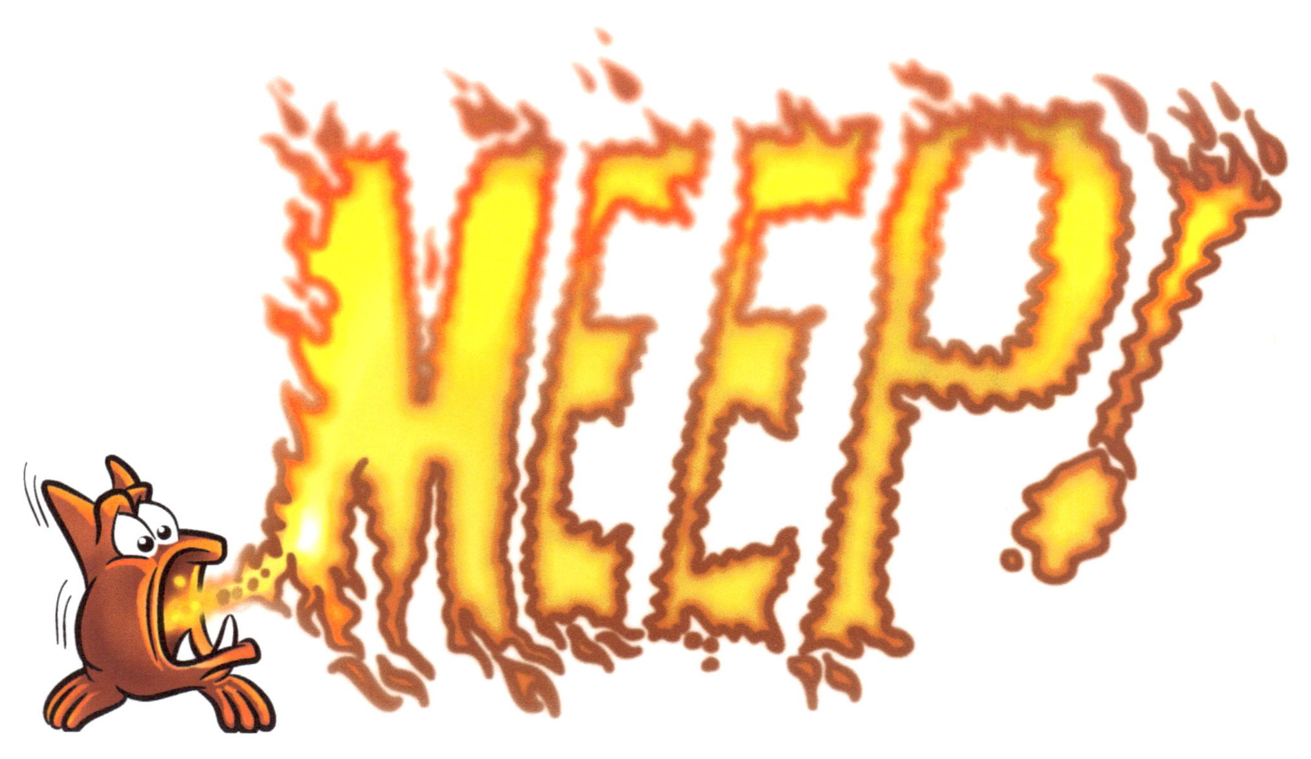

A red impish infant who "MEEPS" a bright flame.

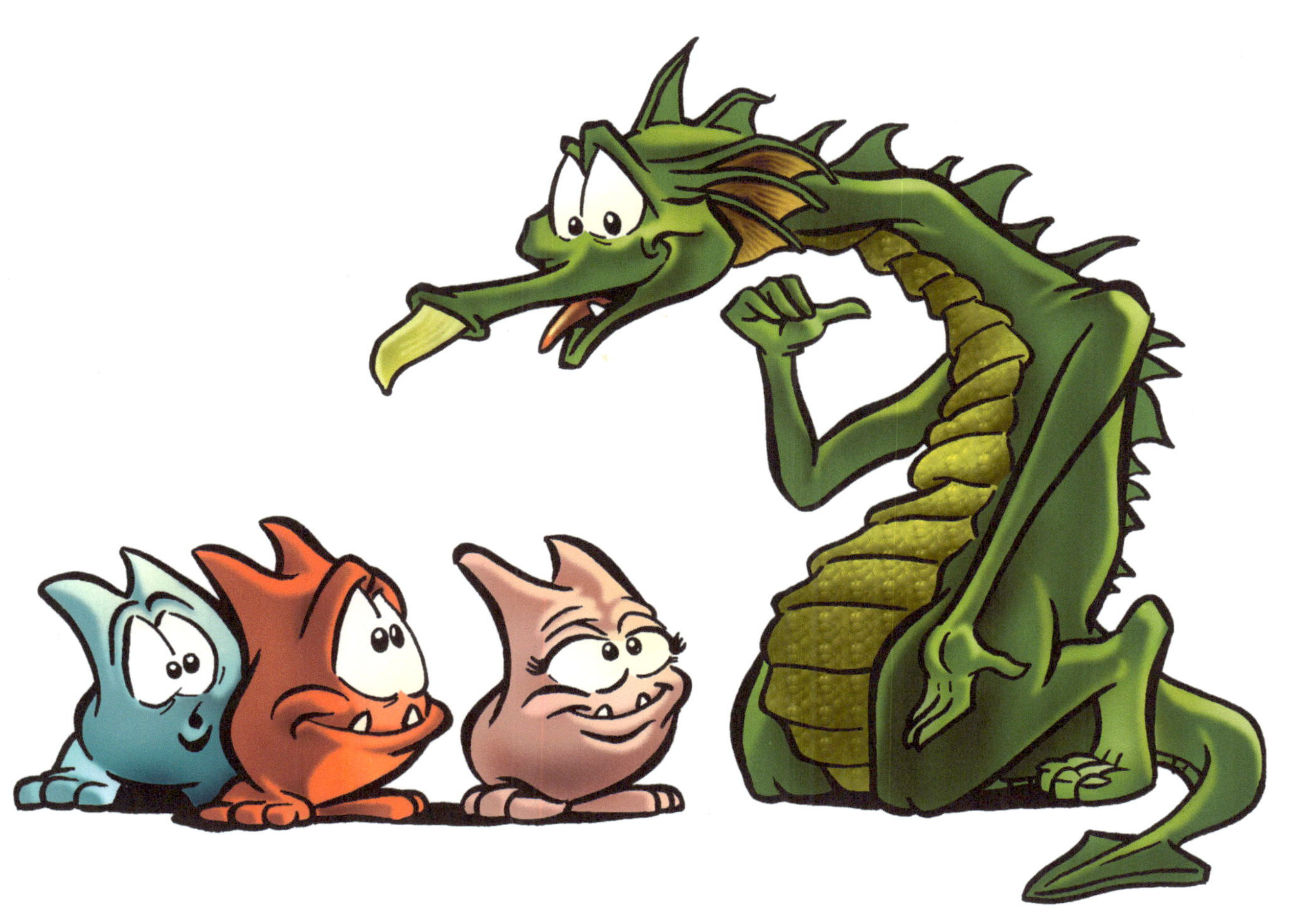

It is one of the many Yets that you shall meet,

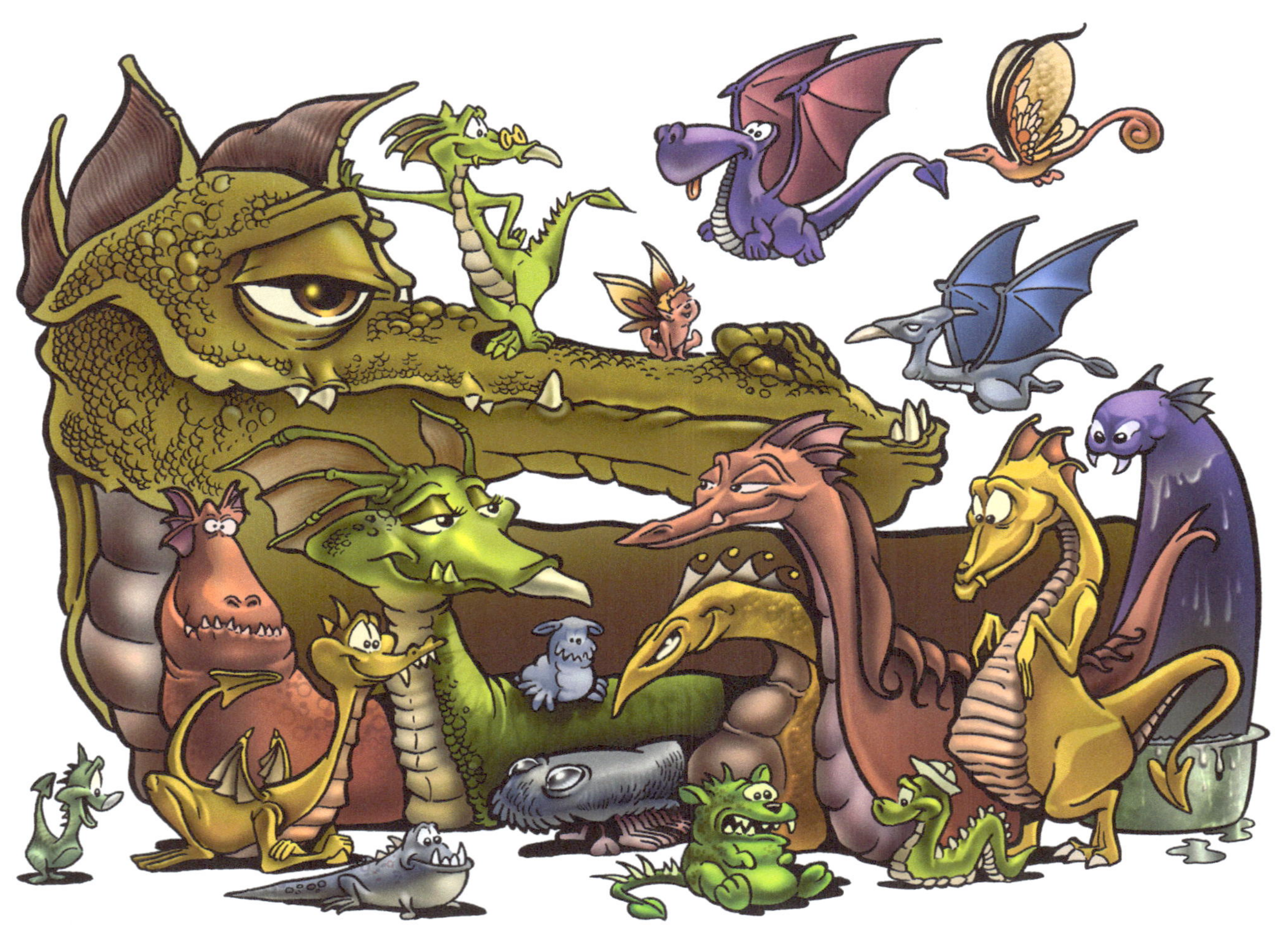

All of them different... all of them neat!

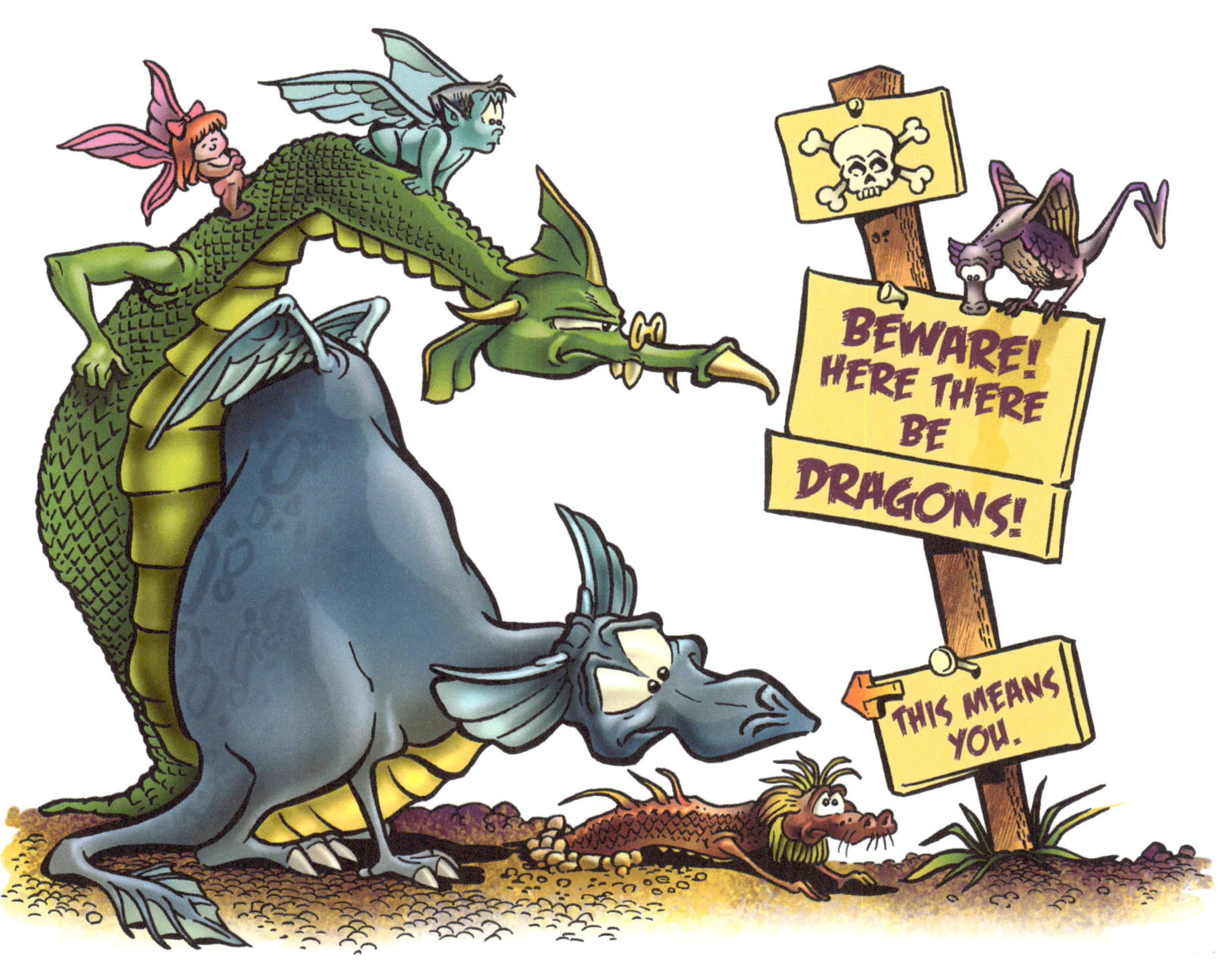

Men call them Dragons,
because they look mean.

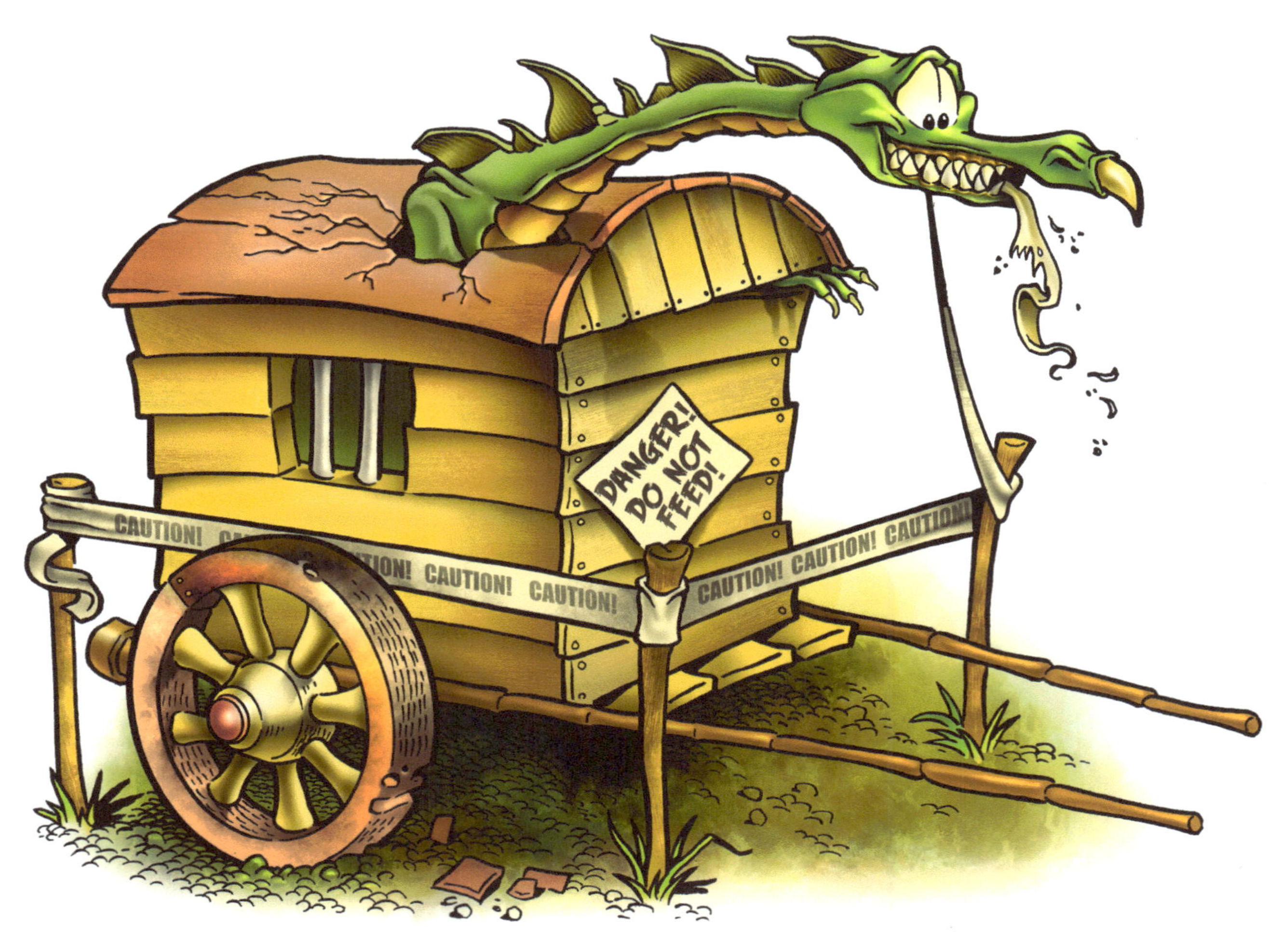

Men fear them and fight them
and call them unclean.

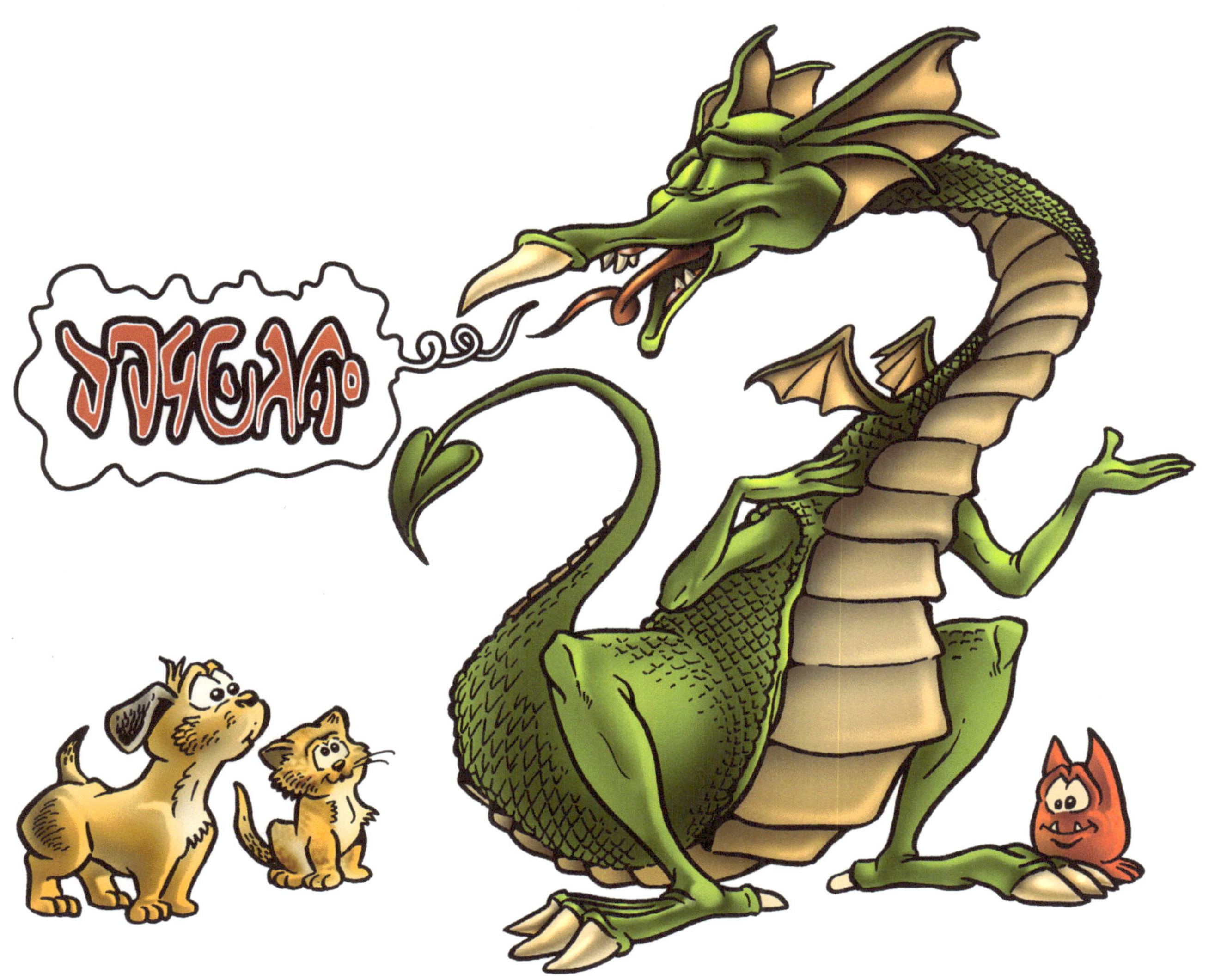

You can not pronounce the name of this weird pet.

So these things had no name...
that is, as of

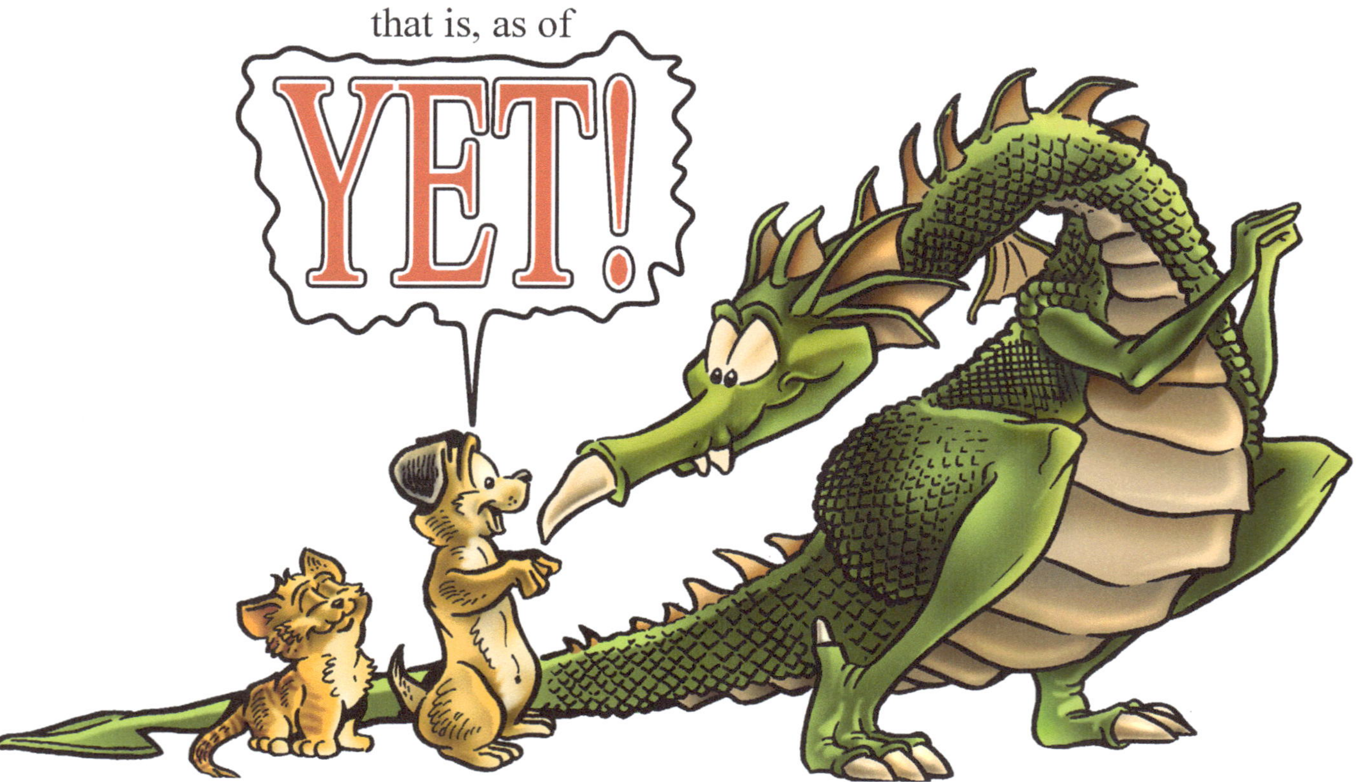

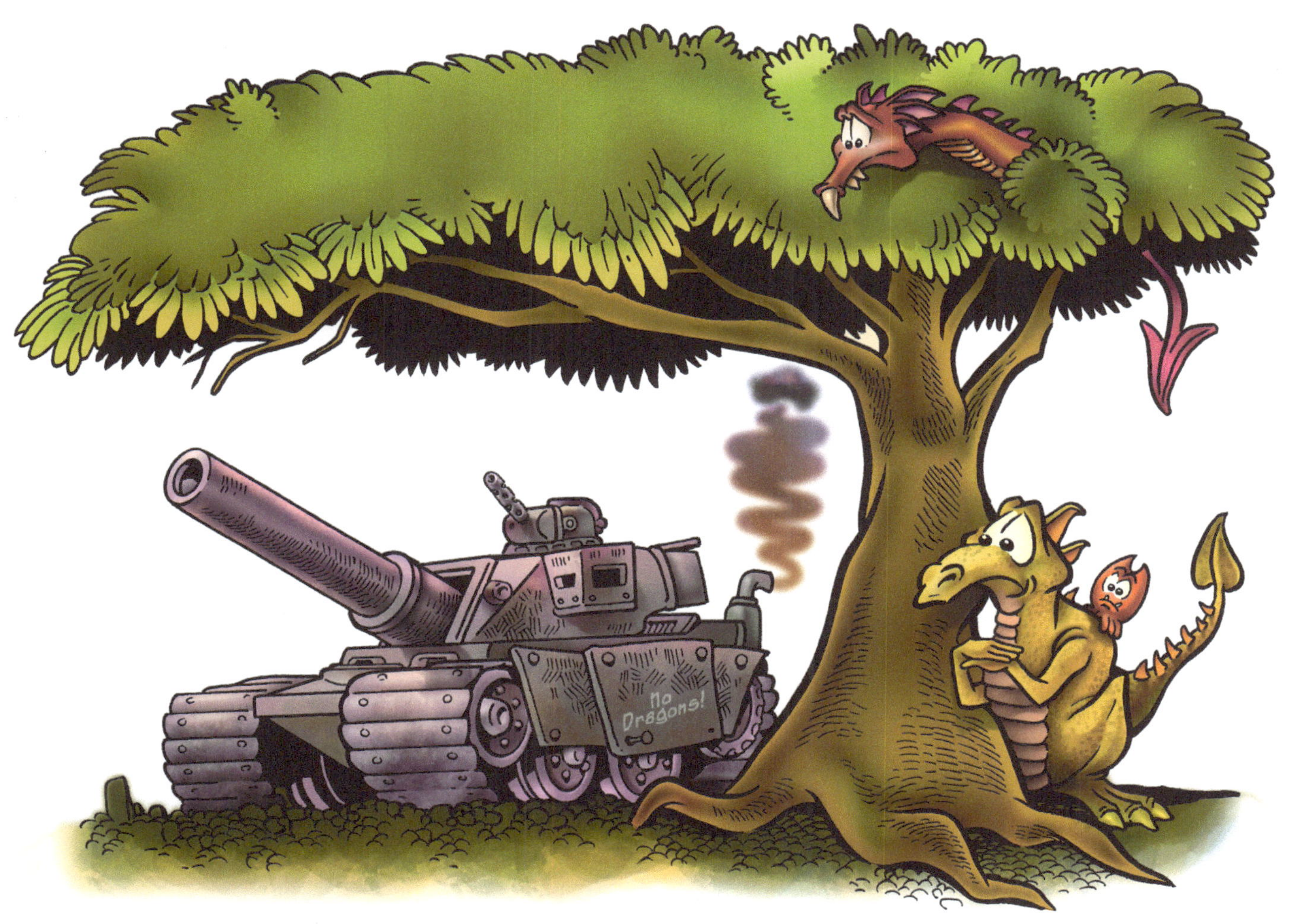

But the Yets need friends,
and the men want more war,

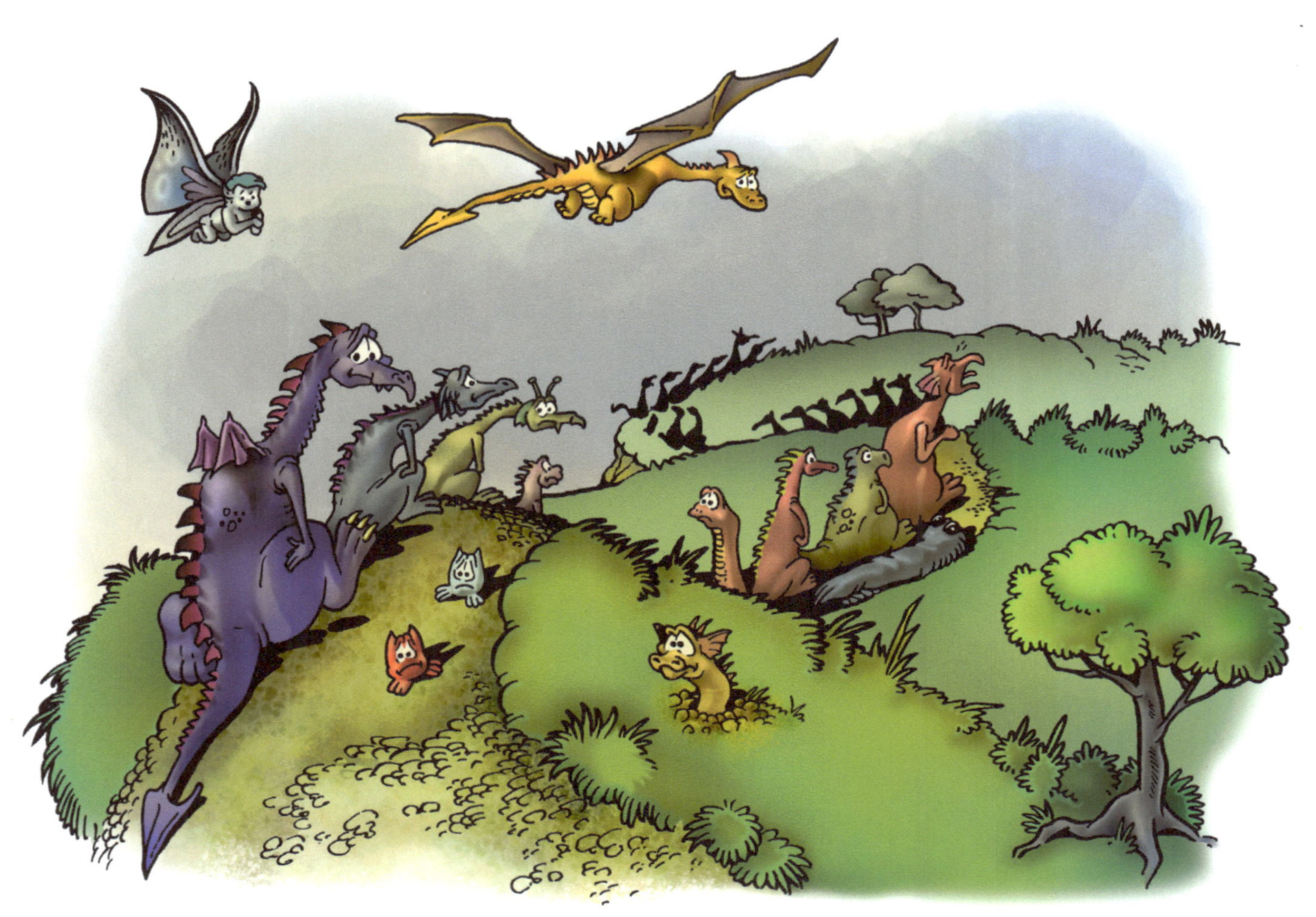

So the Yets left us alone, to return nevermore!

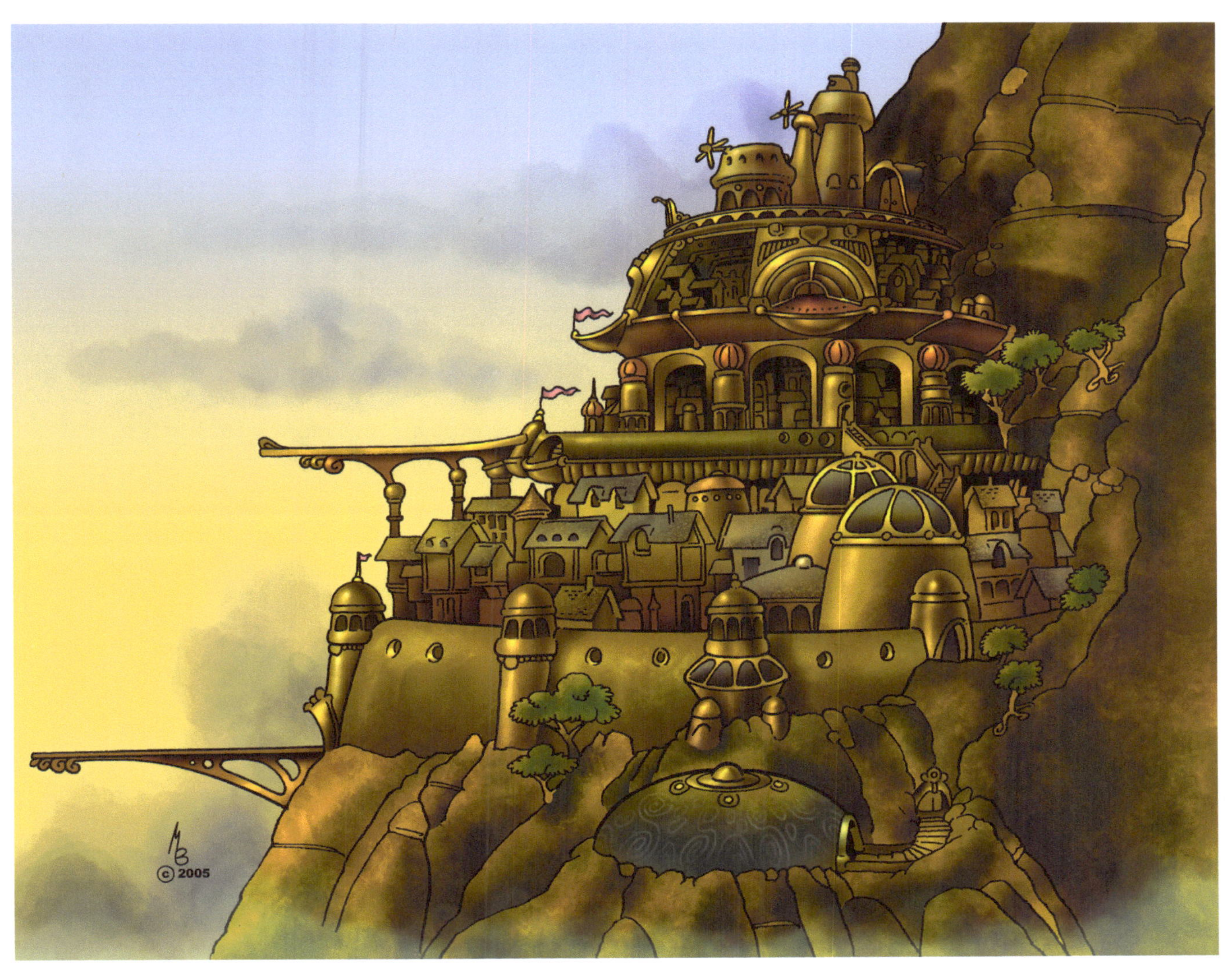

They have a new world, they hid from mankind.

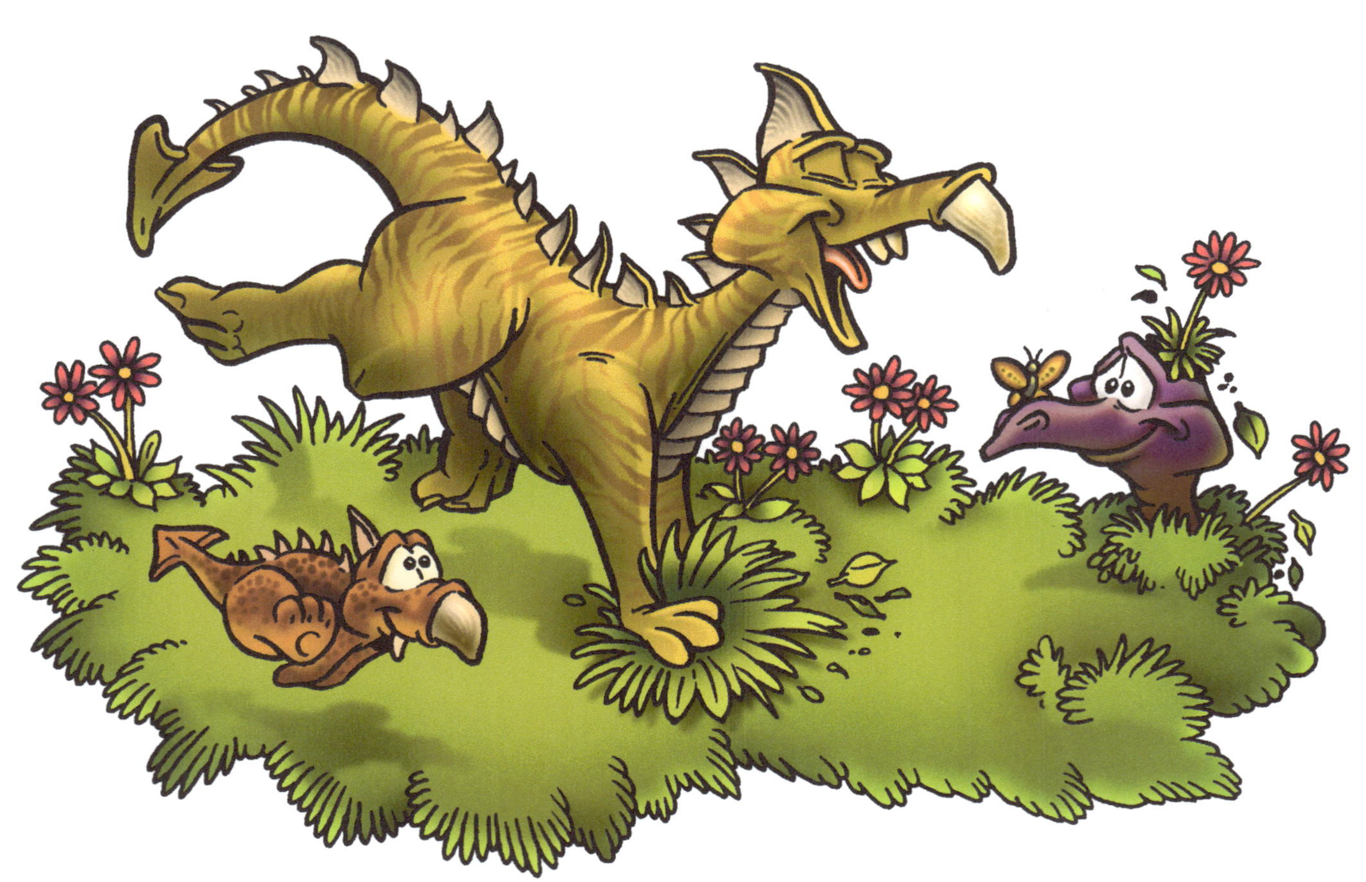

Where all Yets are equal, and live unconfined.

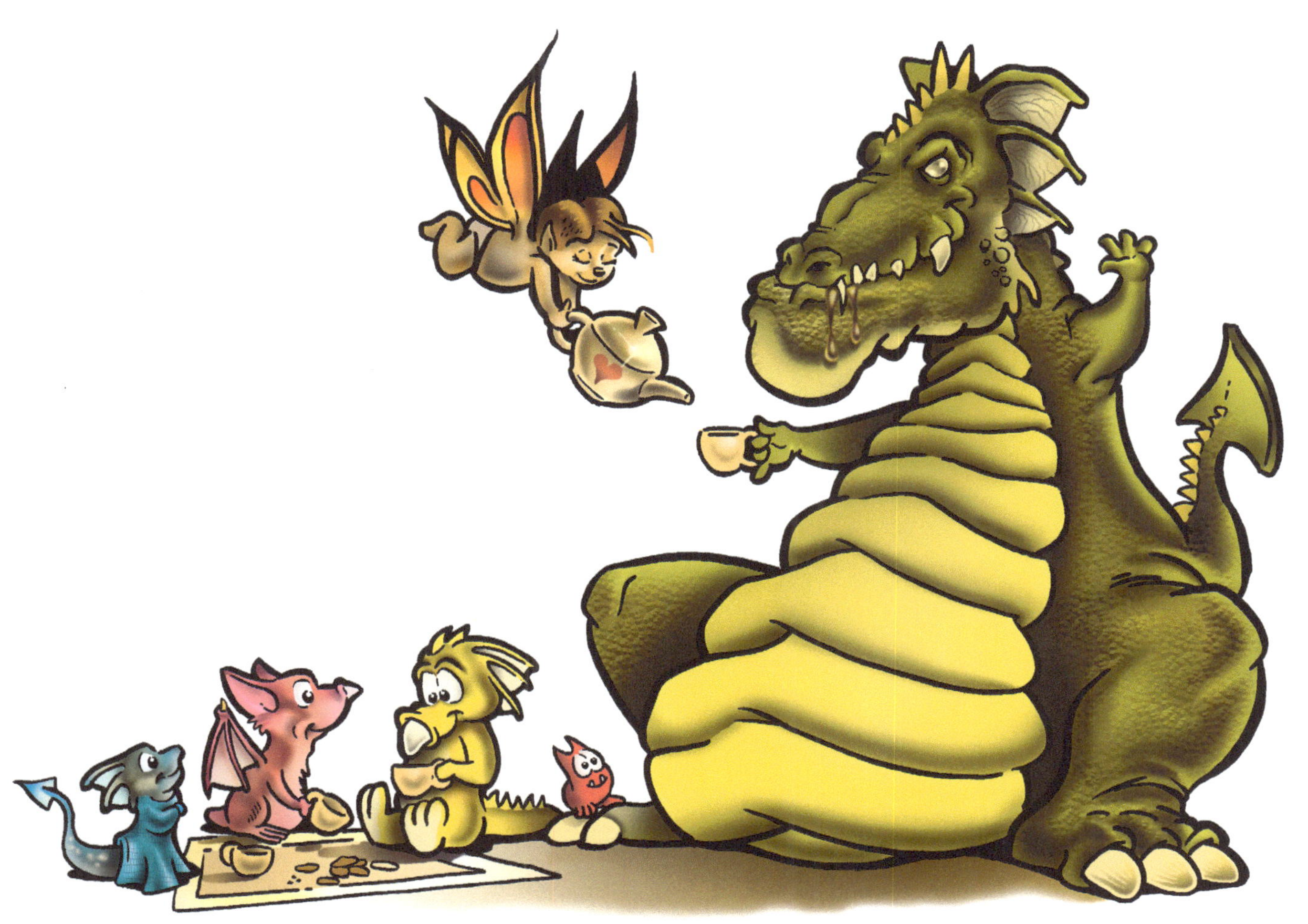

Some of these Yets are as large as a house.

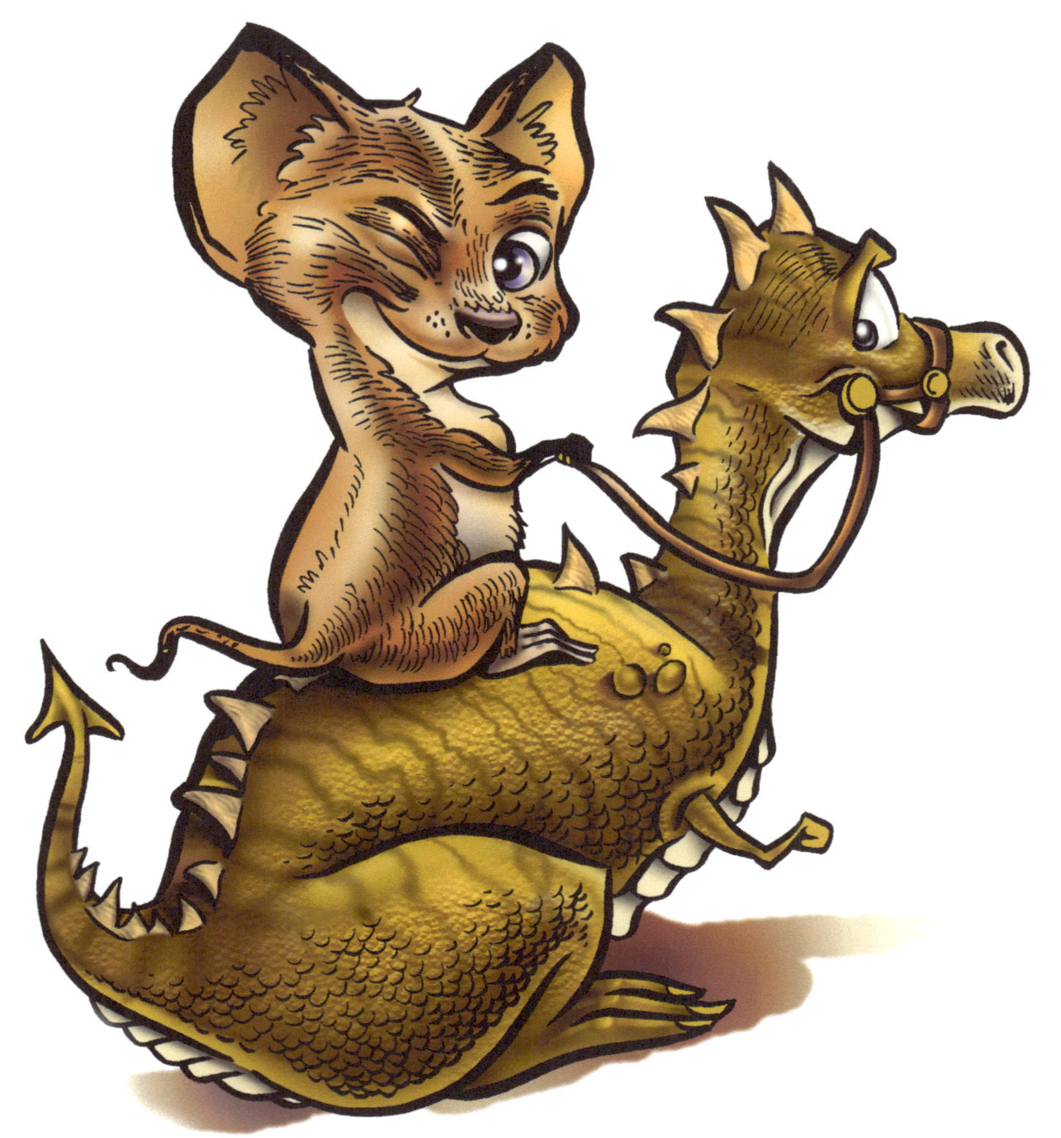

Some of these Yets are as small as a mouse.

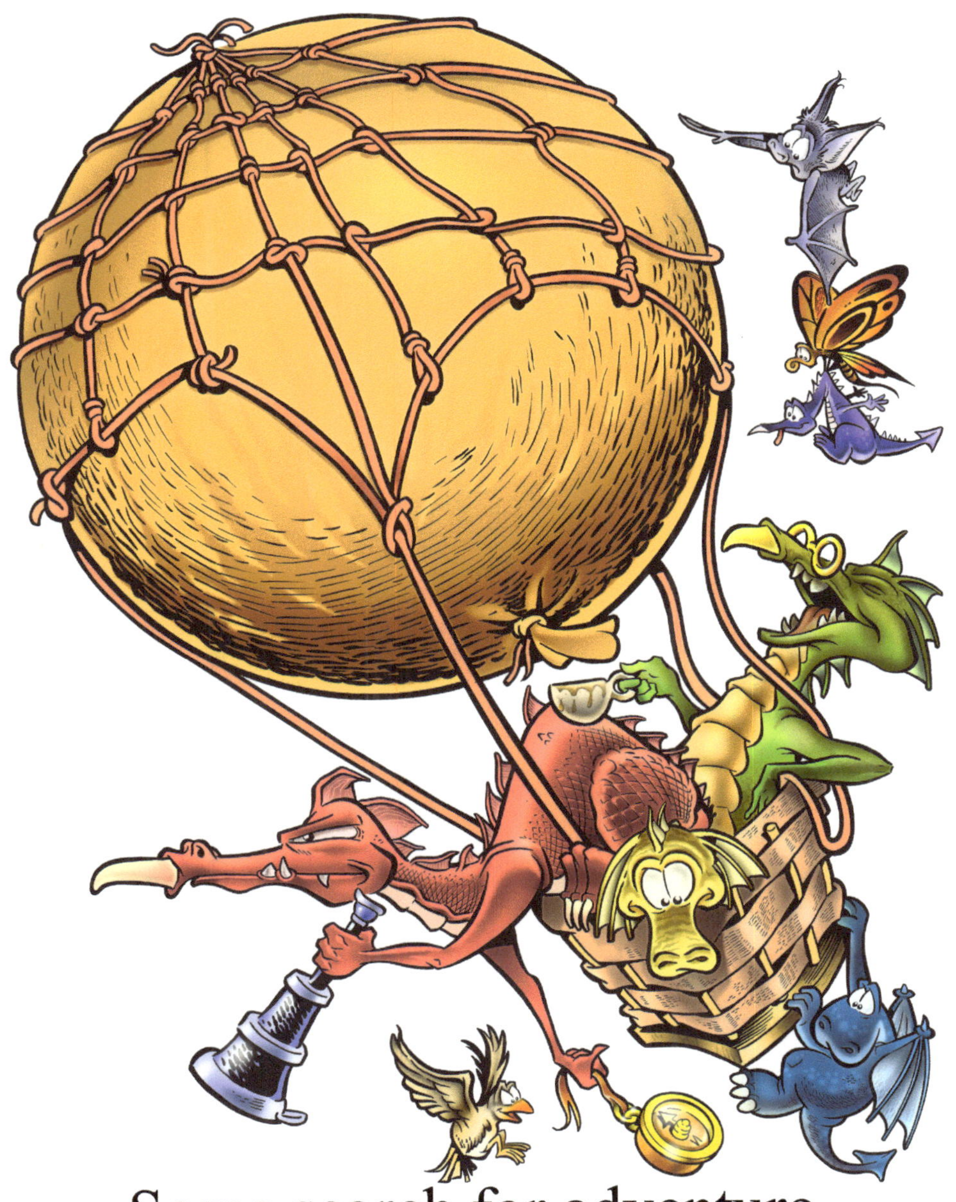

Some search for adventure,

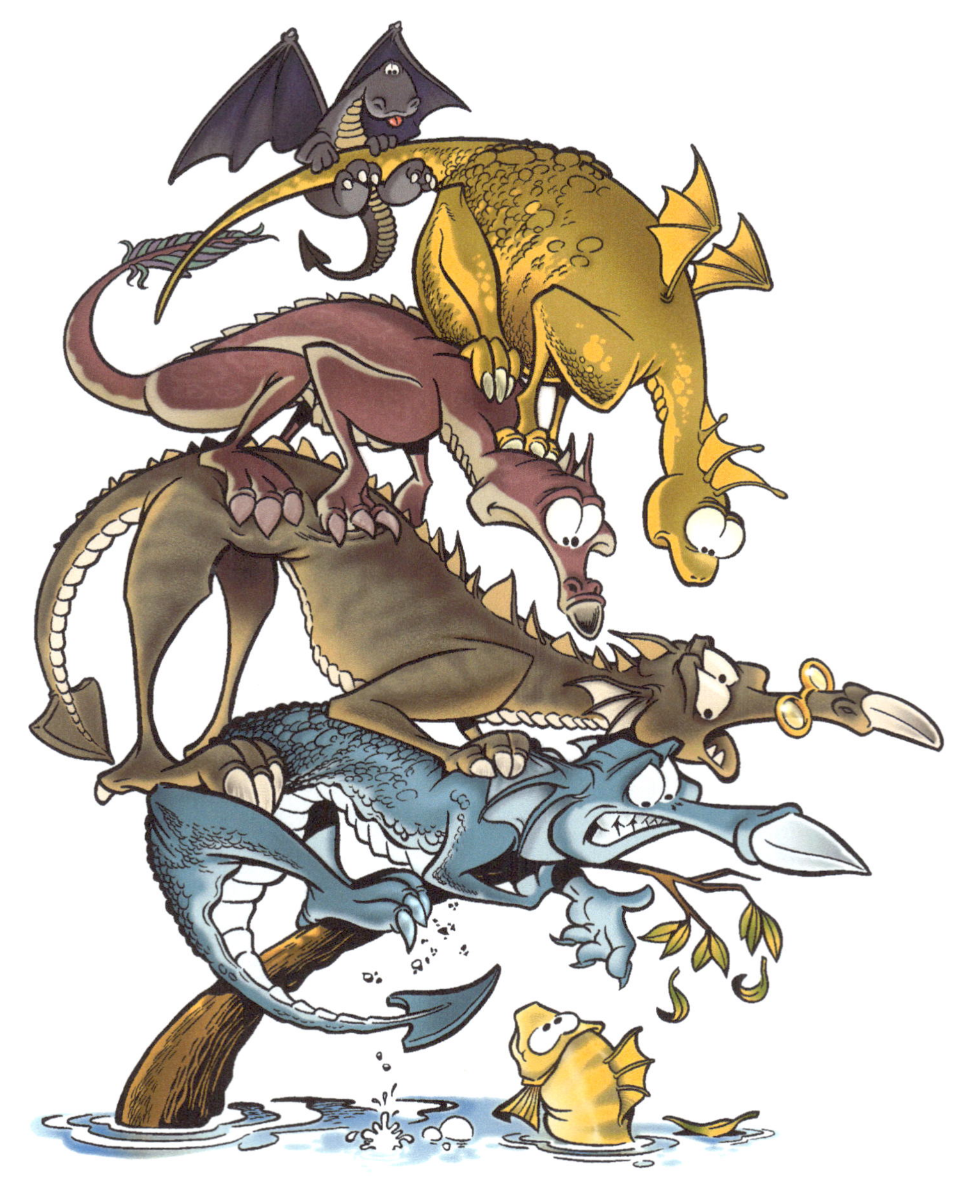

Some Yets are afraid.

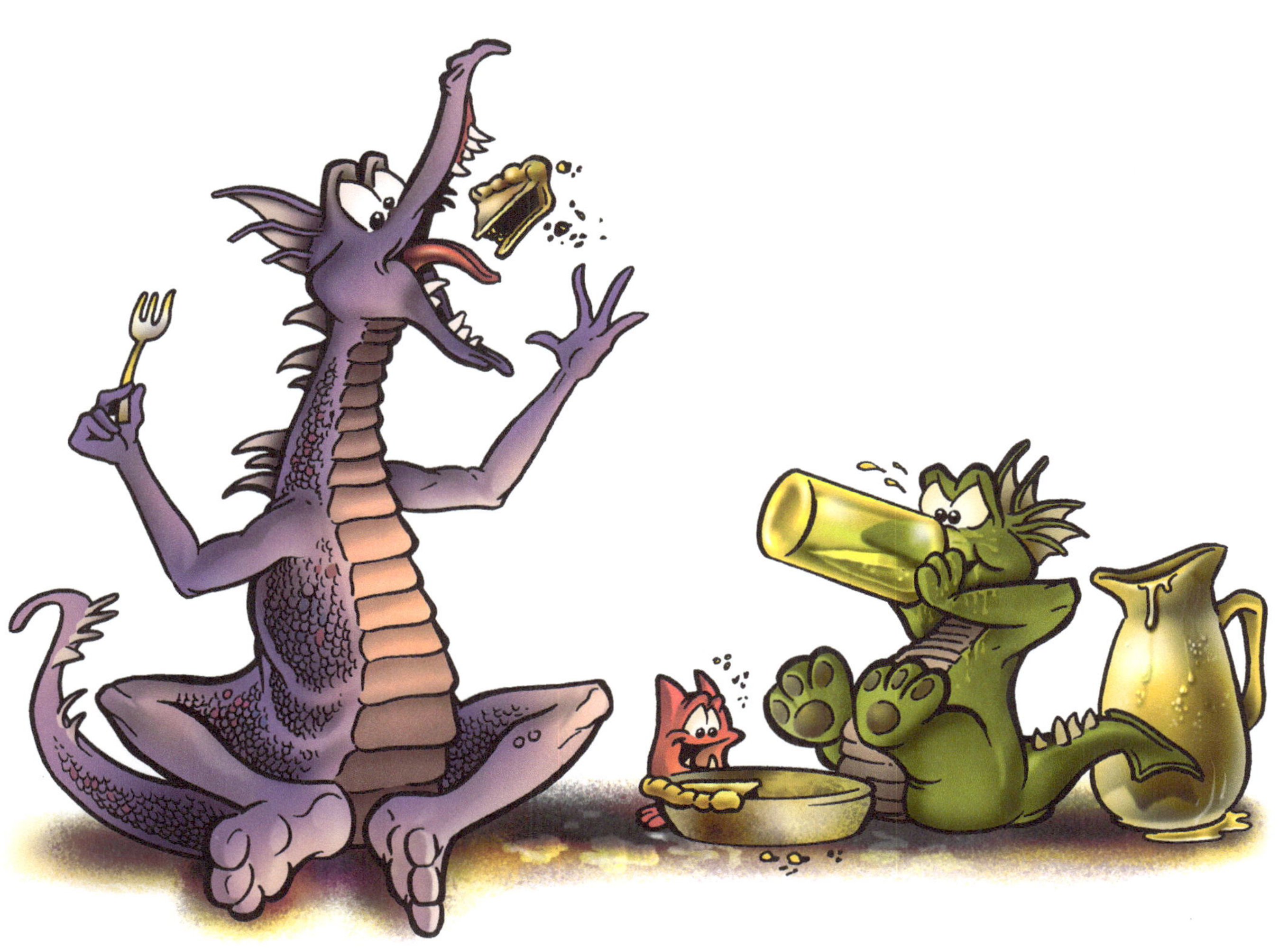

Some like to eat pie and drink lemonade.

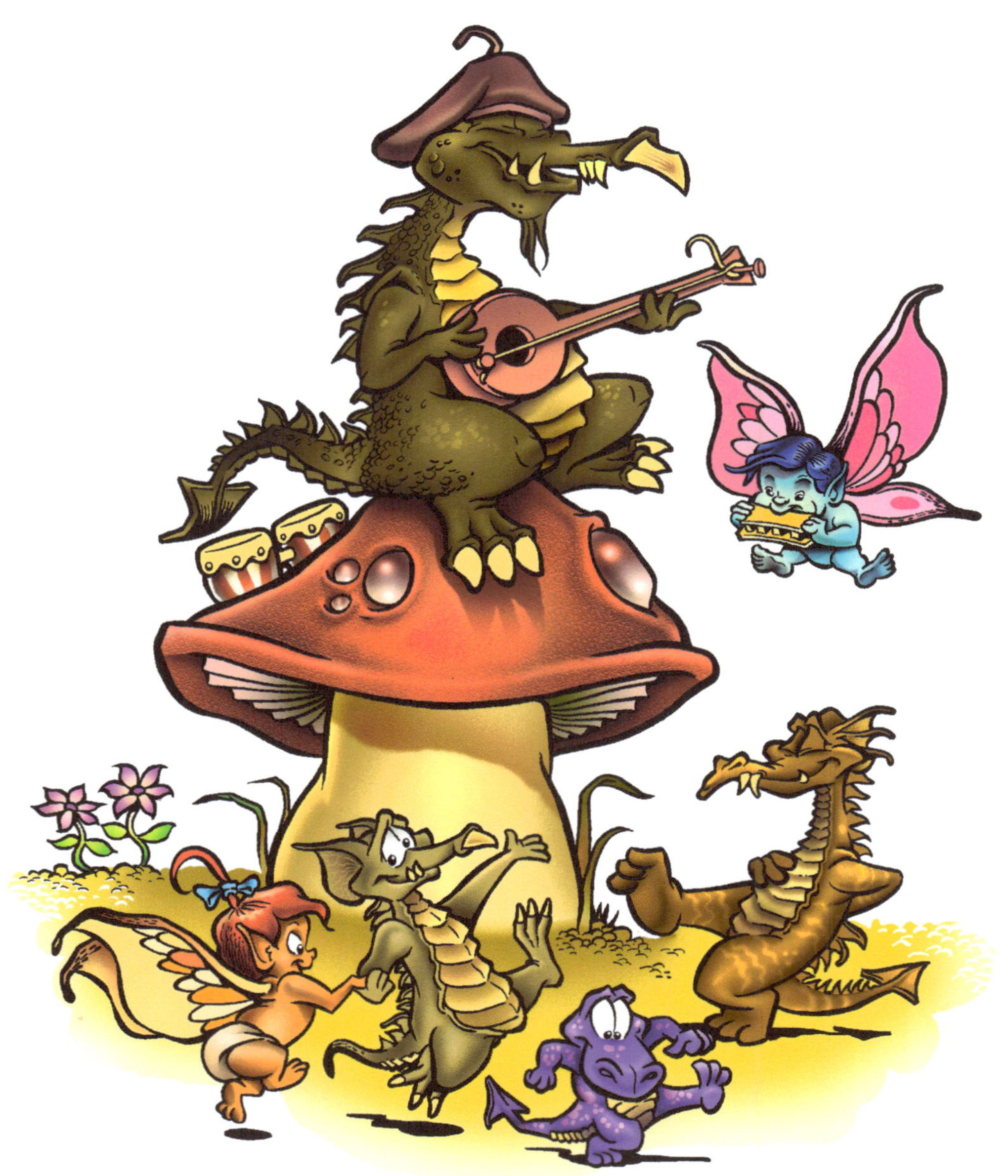

Some Yets play cool jazz,

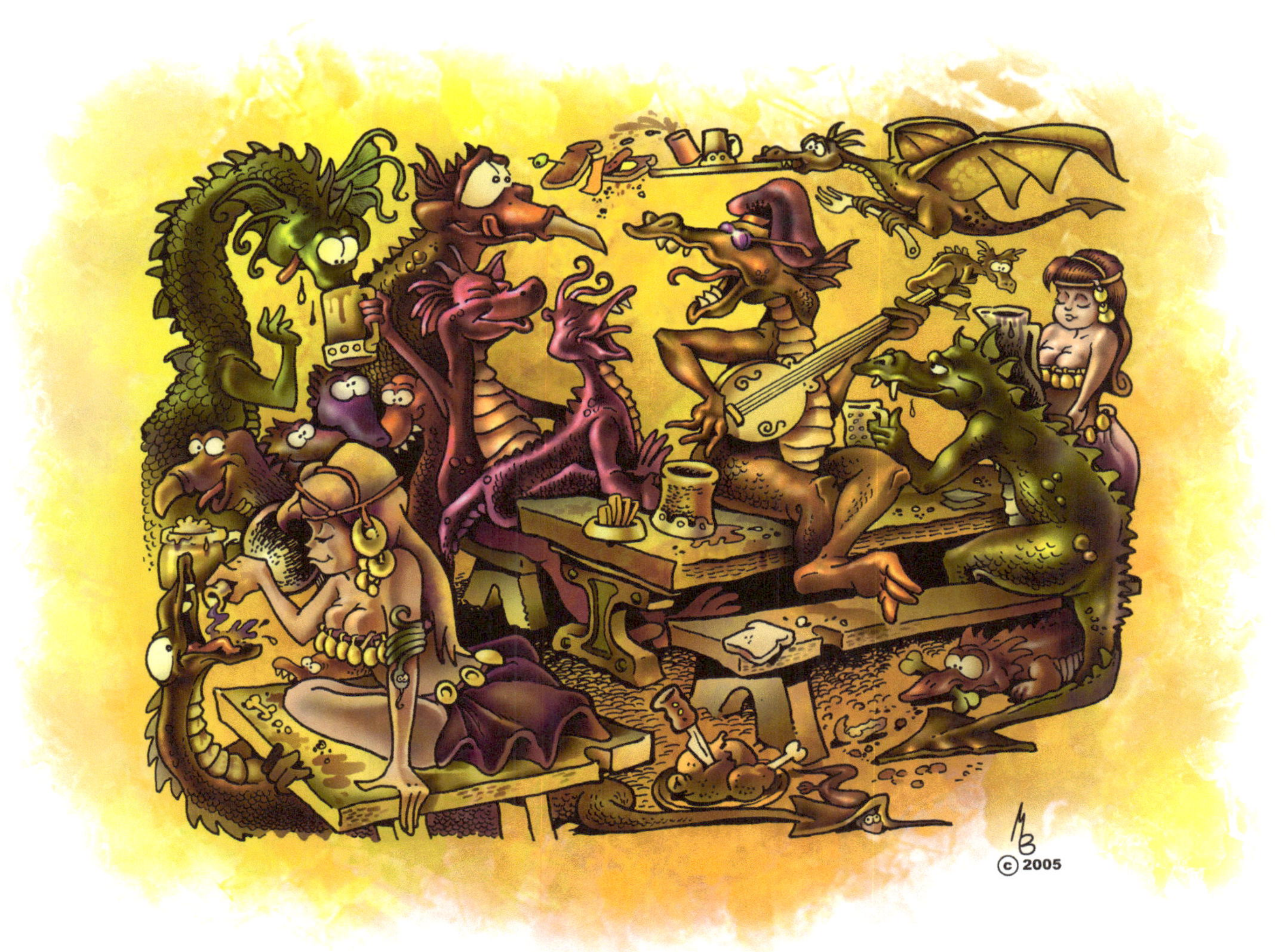

and party all night.

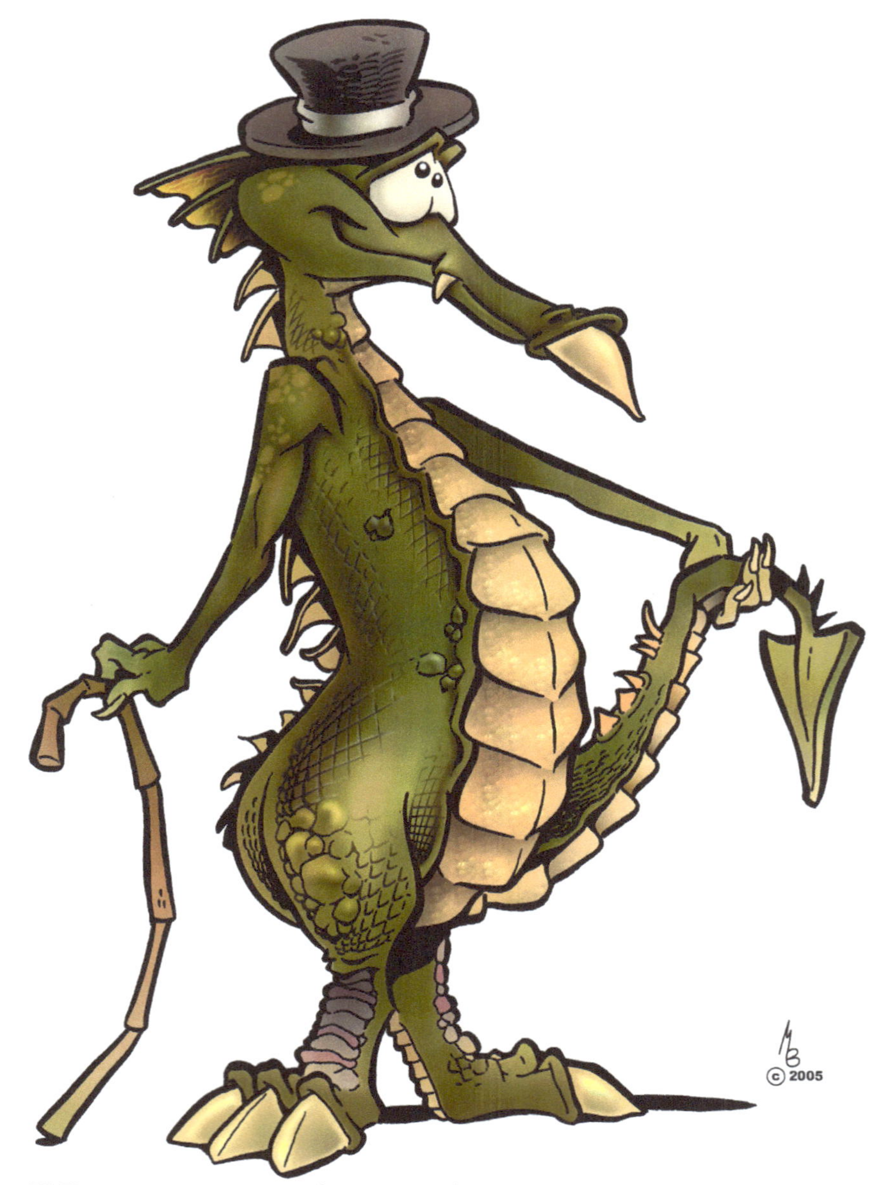

Some Yets are cultured and are quite polite.

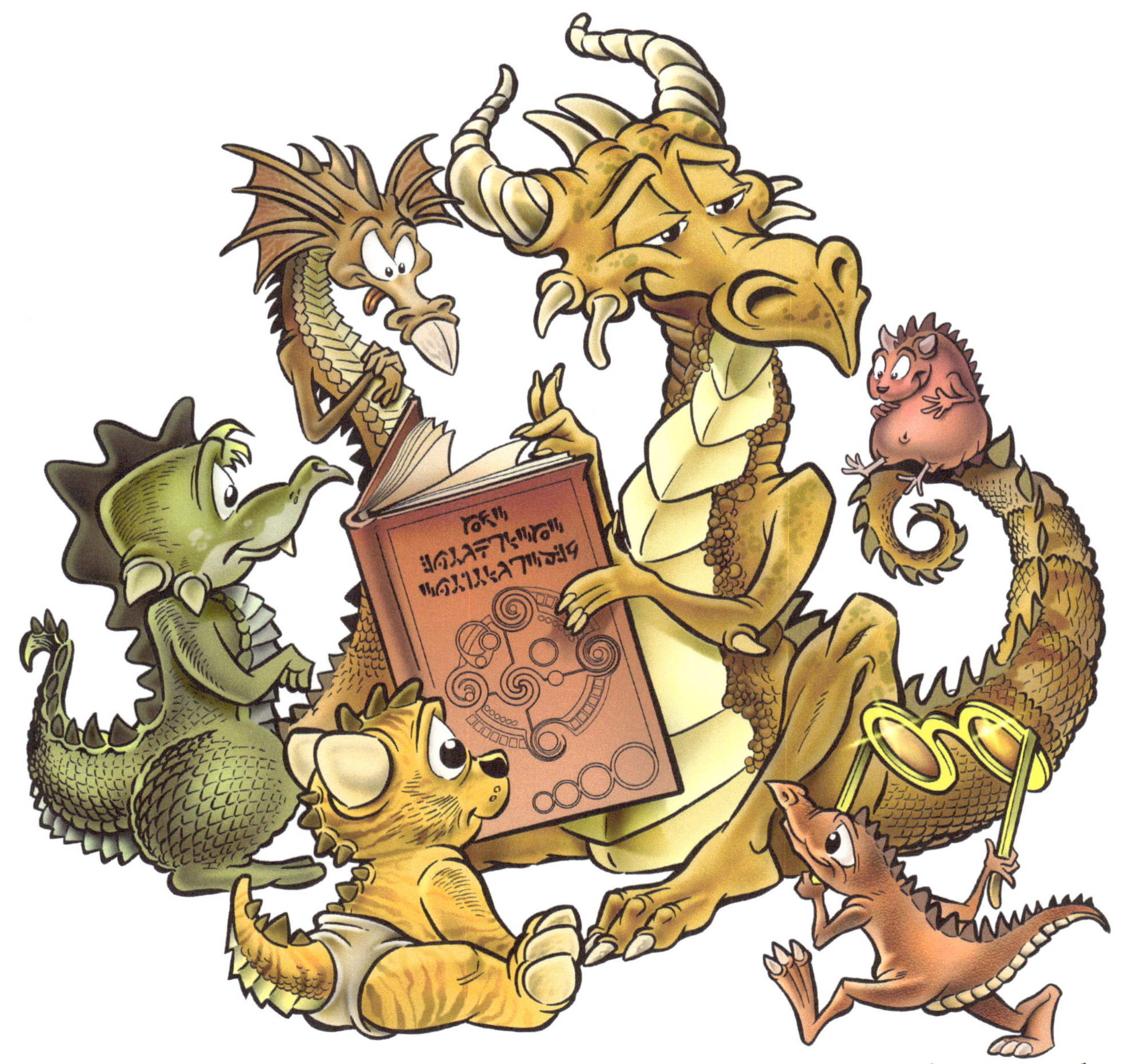

Some Yets found books, so they learn to be cool.

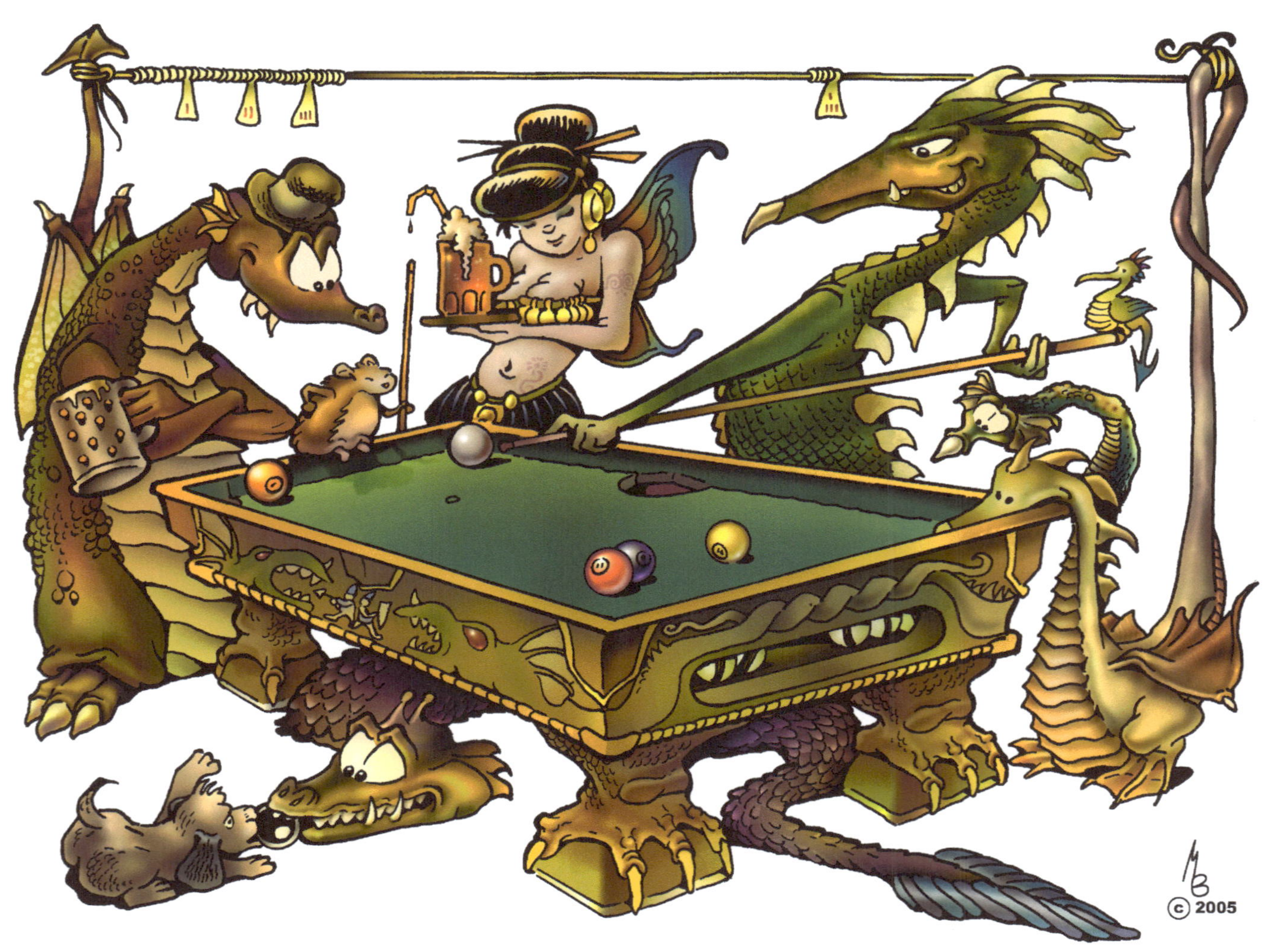

Some learn by hard knocks, and play lots of pool.

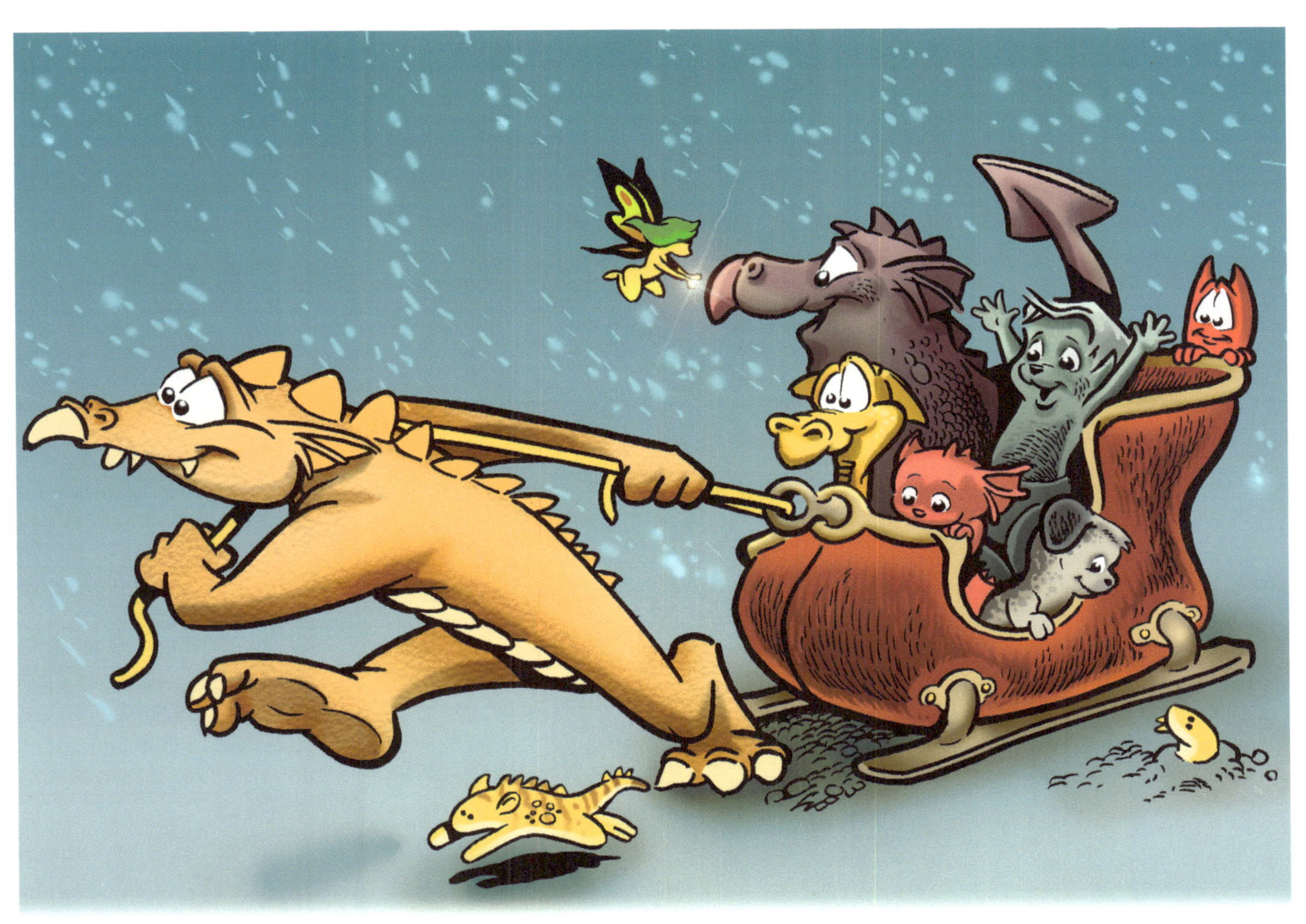

Some Yets like the snow,

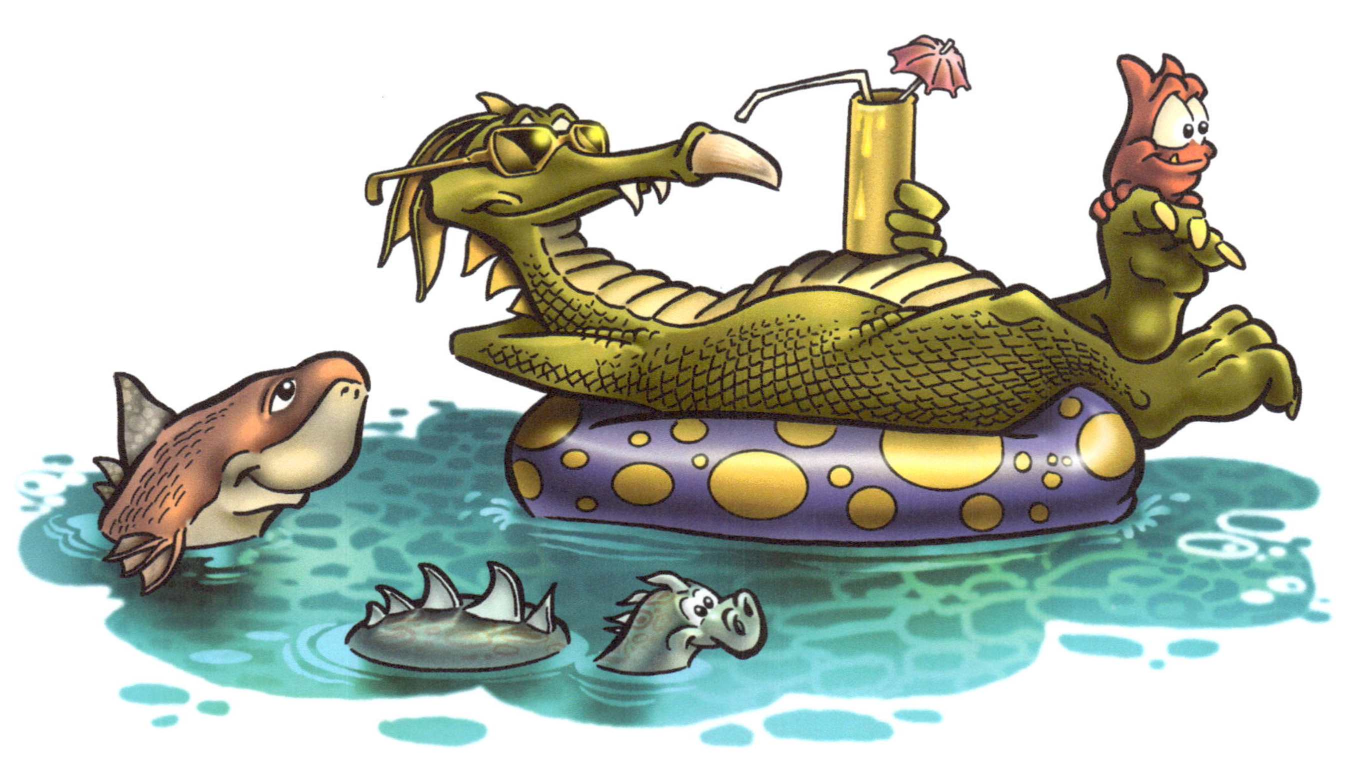

Some Yets bask in the sun.

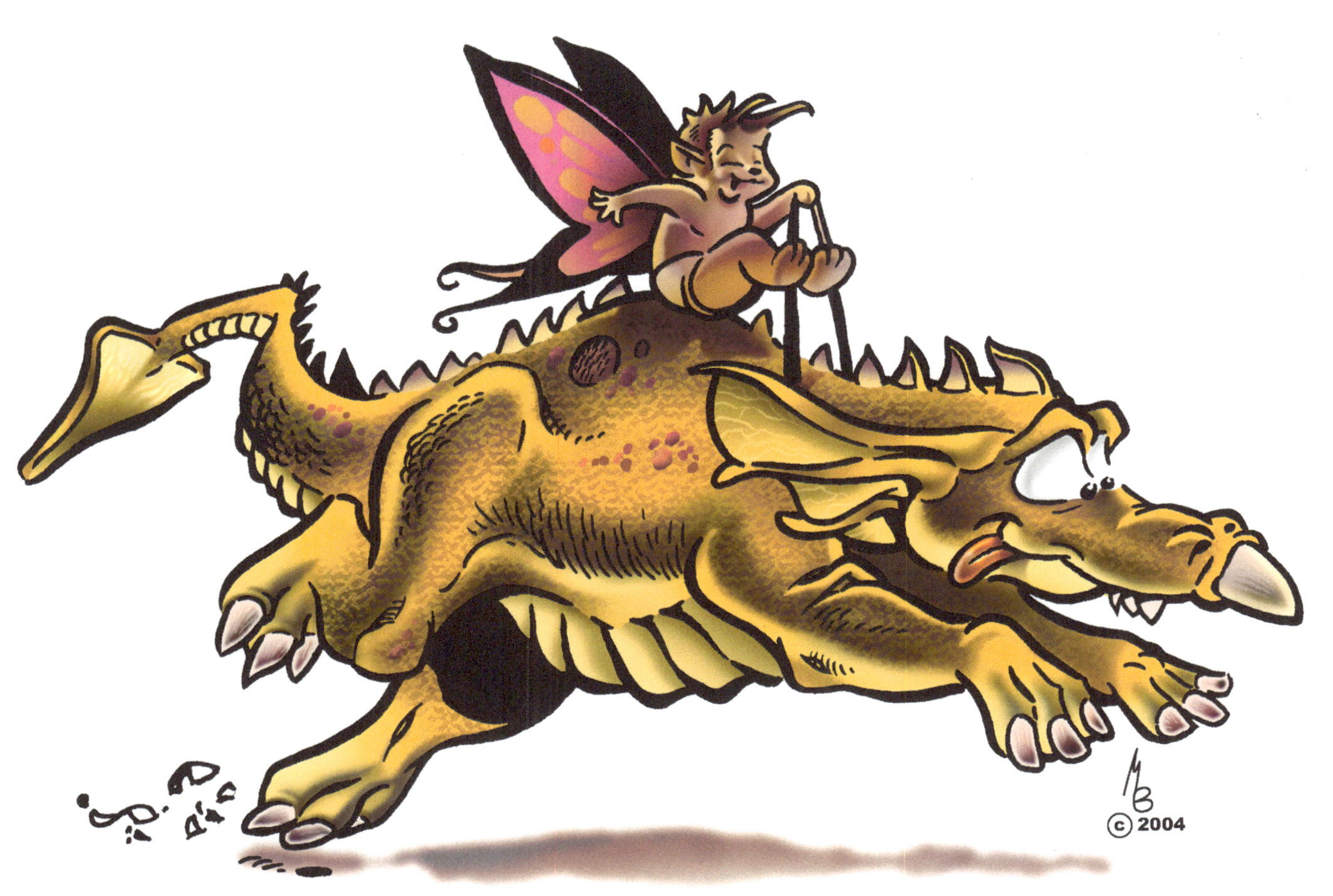

Some Yets just like to run and have fun.

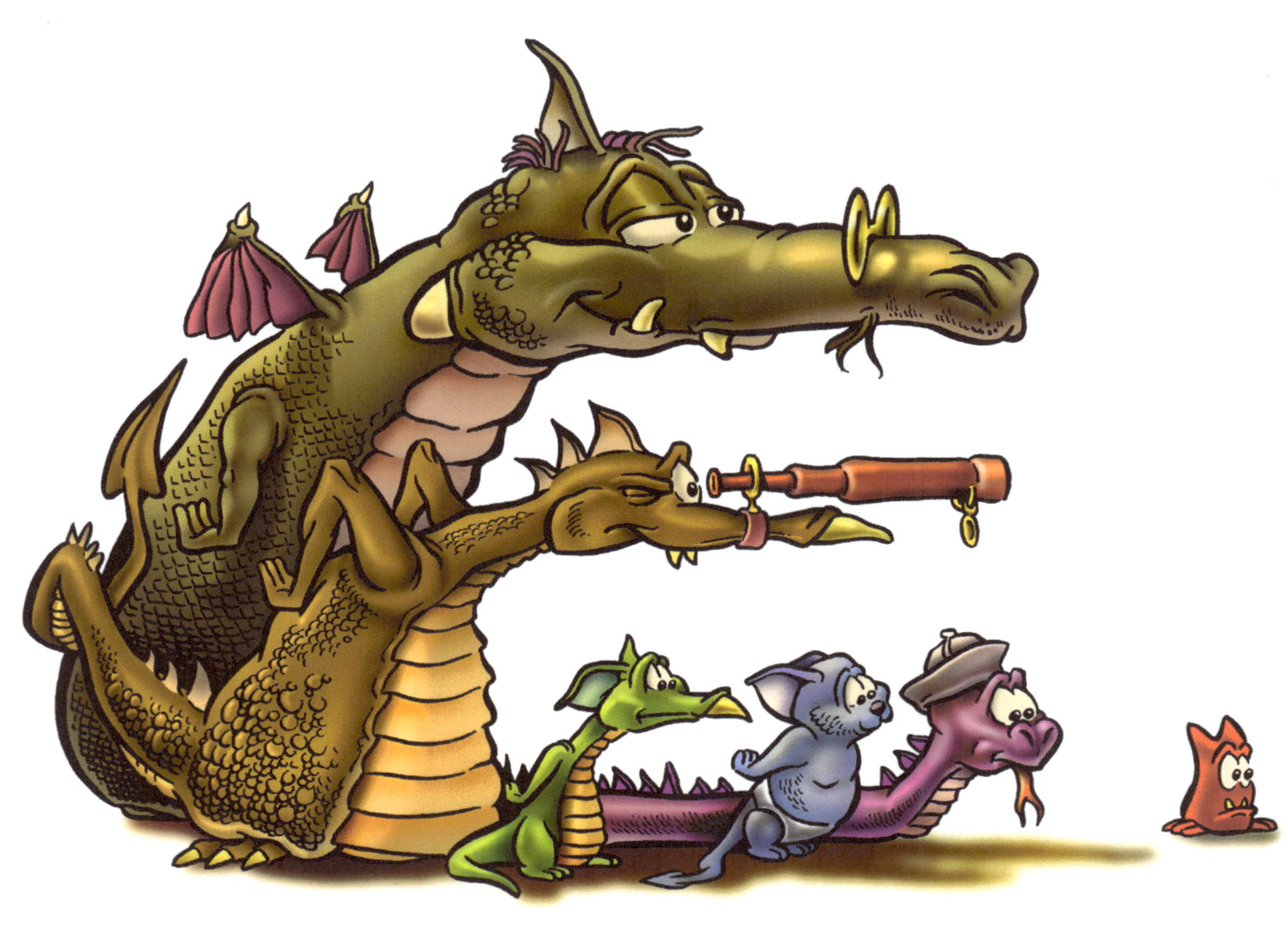

But something is missing, as soon you will spy.

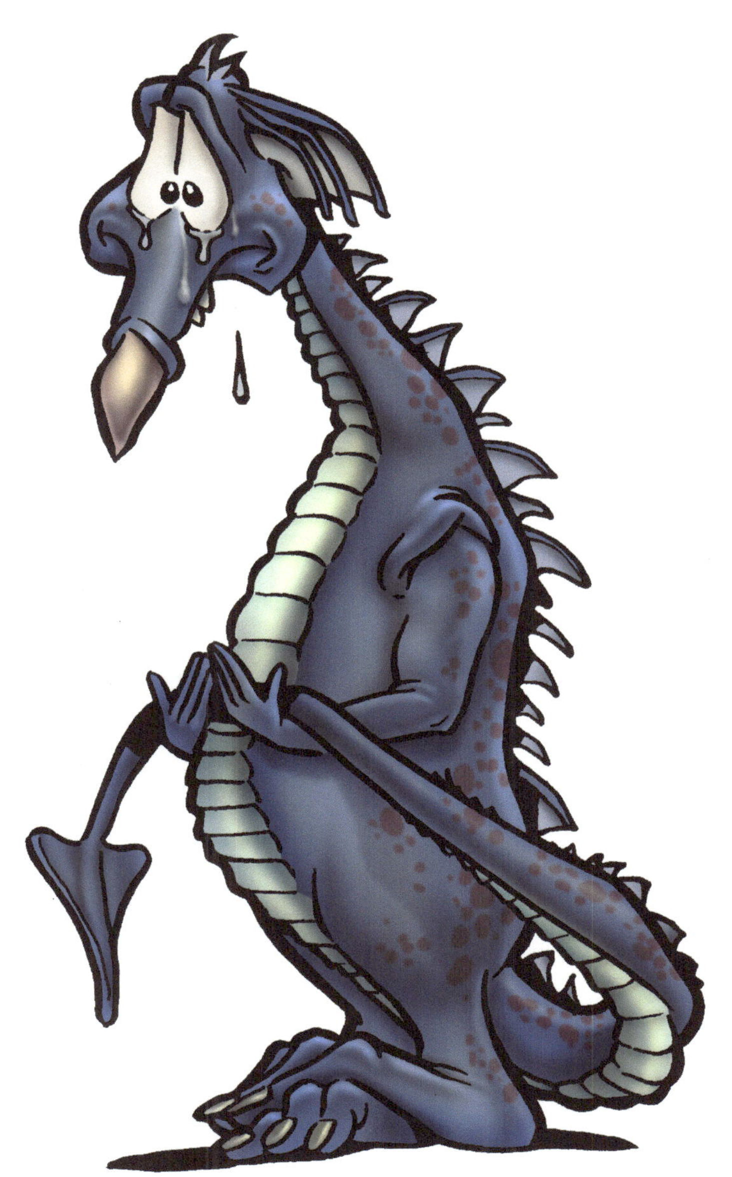

That thing is a friend, and so the Yets cry...

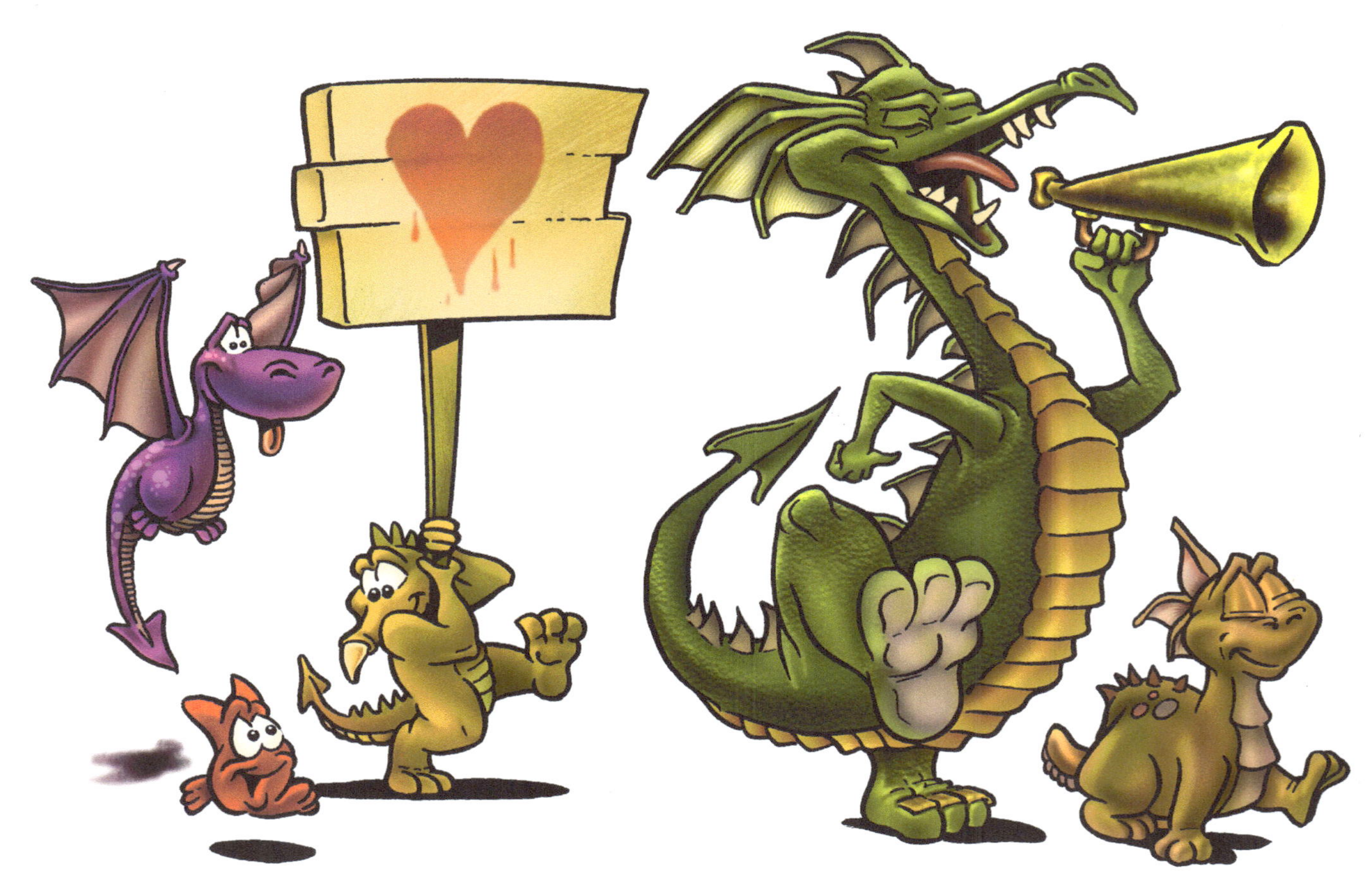

“We’ve lived here too long let us break with the past.
We want to be friends
and we want it to last!”

So what can you do,
for the friends
you've just met?

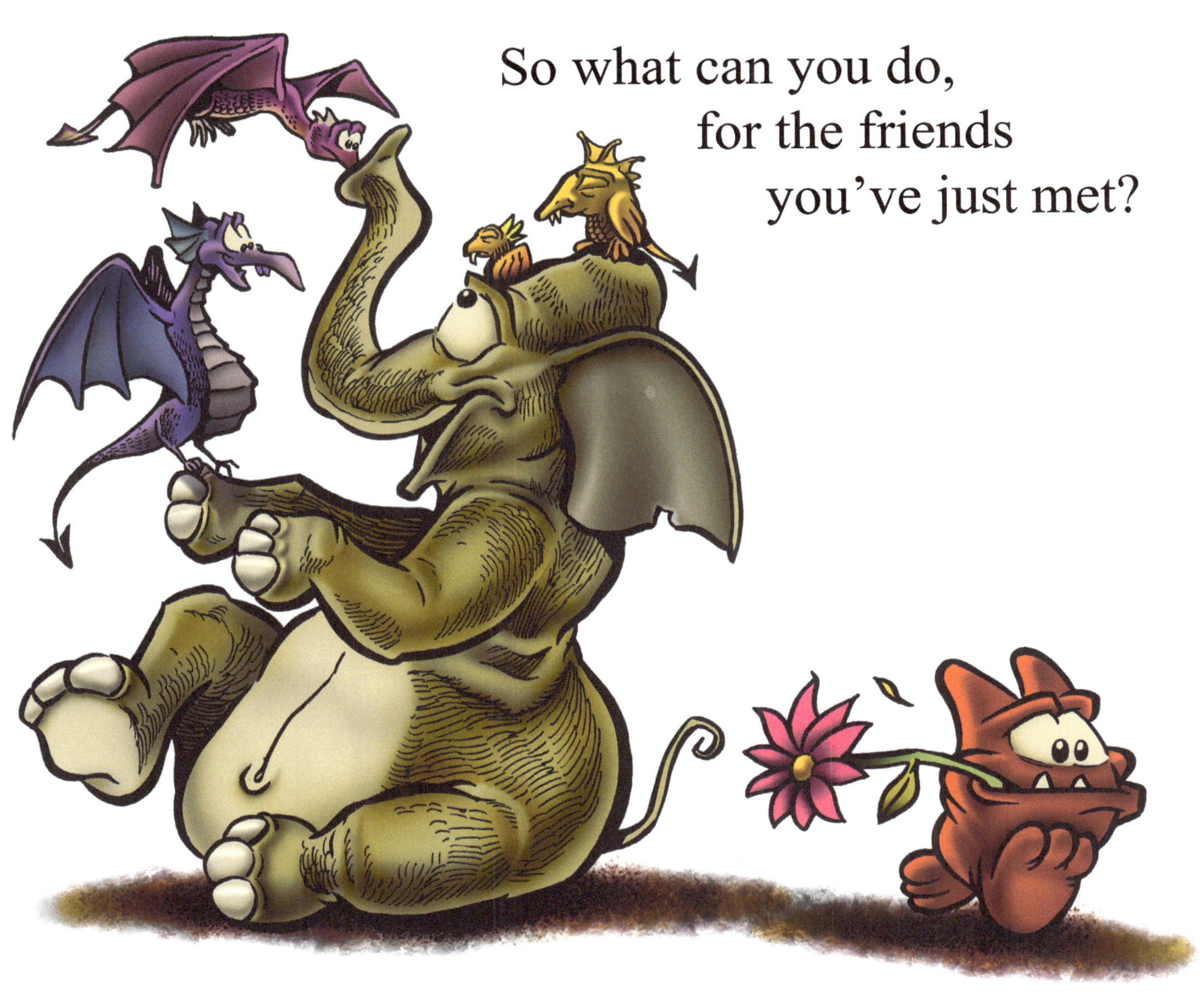

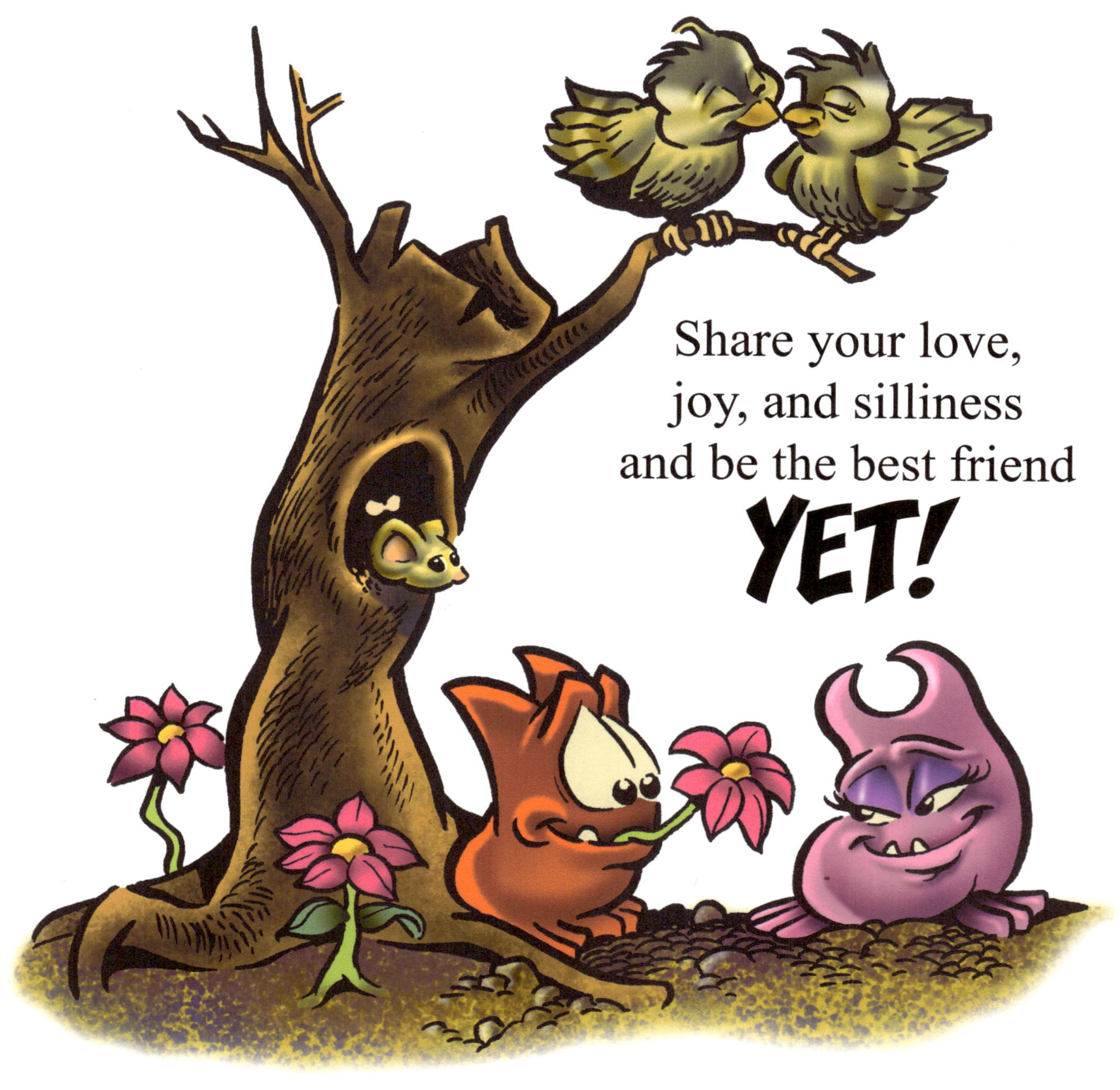
Share your love,
joy, and silliness
and be the best friend
YET!

www.ingramcontent.com/pod-product-compliance
Lightning Source LLC
Chambersburg PA
CBHW042204030726
47602CB00008B/122

* 9 7 8 0 5 7 8 7 1 9 3 5 1 *